Love France

Text and Photographs
Hervé Champollion

Translation
Entreprises 35

Editions OUEST-FRANCE

Administrative France

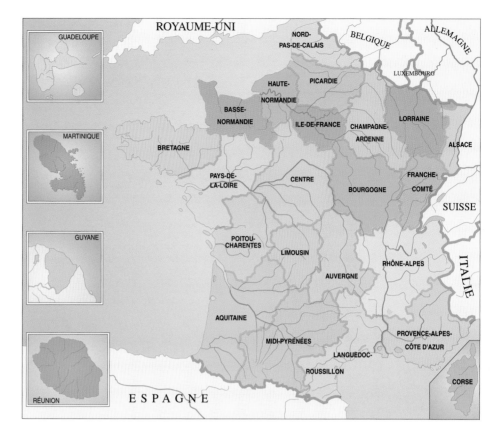

Summary

Physical France

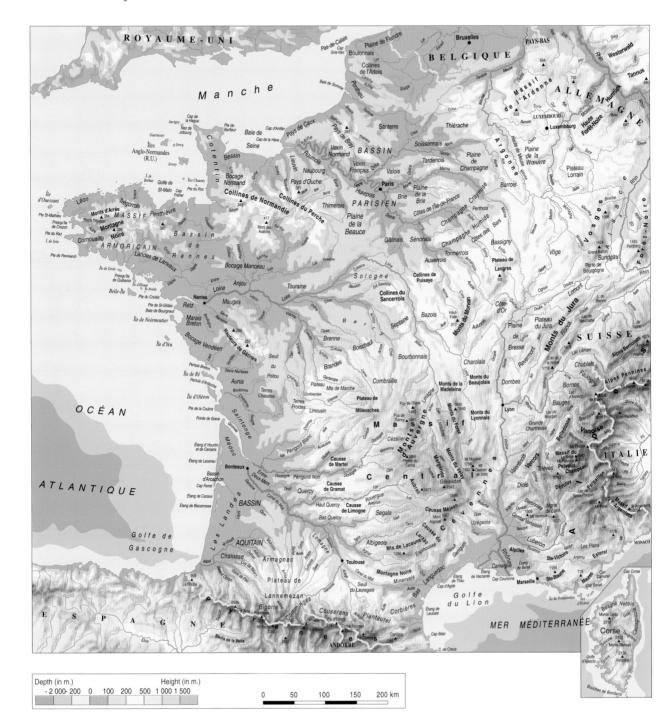

ROYAUME-UNI

BELGIQUE   PAYS-BAS

ALLEMAGNE

Manche

Bruxelles

Massif de l'Ardenne

LUXEMBOURG

Luxembourg   Haute Forêt-Noire

Plaine de la Wœuvre

Plateau Lorrain

Pas-de-Calais   Plaine de Flandre
Cap Gris-Nez   Boulonnais
Baie de Somme   Collines de l'Artois
                 Ponthieu
Cap de la Hague Pays de Caux   Santerre   Thiérache
Nez de Jobourg   Cap d'Antifer   Soissonnais
Baie de   Cap de la Hève Pays de Bray   Plaine de
Seine   Roumois   Vexin   Tardenois   Champagne
Bessin   Neubourg   Normand BASSIN   Valois
Cotentin   Lieuvin   Vexin   Plaine de
                 Pays d'Oureh Français Paris   la Brie   Barrois
Bocage   Collines de Normandie   Hurepoix Brie
Normand   Collines du Perche   PARISIEN   Côtes de l'Île-de-France
Golfe de St-Malo Thimerais   Plaine de la   Champagne Crayeuse
                 Beauce   Sénonais   Champagne Humide   Bassigny
Léon Trégorrois MASSIF Penthièvre Gâtinais   Côtes des Bars   Plateau de
Monts d'Arrée   Auxerrois   Tonnerrois   Langres
Montagne Noire   Bassin de Rennes   Collines de   Vôge   Porte de
Cornouaille   Bocage Manceau   Puisaye   Bourgogne
ARMORICAIN   Landes de Lanvaux Sologne Collines du   Côte-d'Or
                 Anjou Touraine   Sancerrois
Belle-Île Nantes Mauges Berry   Bazois   Monts du Morvan Plaine de Bresse
                 Retz   Autunois   Plateau du Jura
Marais Breton   Hauteurs de Gâtines Brenne Septaine   Charolais
Bocage Vendéen   Seuil du Poitou Boischaut   Monts du
                 Aunis Terres Chaudes Brandes Bourbonnais Beaujolais Dombes
Île de Ré   Terres Froides   Combraille   Monts de la Madeleine
Île d'Oléron   Plateau de Mts de Marche   Monts du Forez
                 Limousin   Millevaches Puy de Dôme Monts du Lyonnais
OCÉAN   Pte de la Coubre   Massif Lyon   Grande Chartreuse
                 Pointe de Grave Périgord Blanc d'Auvergne Monts du Velay Vercors
ATLANTIQUE   Étang d'Hourtin Causse de Martel   Cézallier Margeride
                 et de Carcans   Causse de Gramat   Central   Diois
Bordeaux   Médoc Périgord Noir Quercy Aubrac   Cévennes Dévoluy
                 Bassin d'Arcachon   Haut Quercy Causse de Limogne Ségala
Golfe de   Cap Ferret   Bas Quercy   Causse Méjean   Alpilles
Gascogne   Étang de Cazaux   Albigeois Larzac Uzégeois Ste-Victoire
                 BASSIN Mts de Lacaune Causse de   Esterel
                 Chalosse AQUITAIN Toulouse Montagne Noire Languedoc
                 Armagnac   Minervois   Camargue   Marseille
                 Plateau de   Seuil du Lauragais Bas Languedoc
                 Lannemezan   Bigorre Corbières   Golfe du Lion
ESPAGNE   Couserans Plantaurel Cap d'Agde
                 Pyrénées   MER MÉDITERRANÉE
ANDORRE

SUISSE

Alpes Bernoises
Lac Léman
Chablais
Faucigny   Alpes Pannines
Bornes
Bauges   Mt Blanc
Grande   Vanoise   ITALIE
Chartreuse
Trièves   Massif du   Chamrousse
Pelvoux
Dévoluy   Massif de l'Argentera

MONACO

Corse
Balagne Nebbio
Monte Cinto
Monte Rotondo
Monte Renoso
Golfe d'Ajaccio
Bouches de Bonifacio

Cap Corse

Depth (in m.)			Height (in m.)					
- 2 000	- 200	0	0	100	200	500	1 000	1 500

0   50   100   150   200 km

Vineyards and Appellations

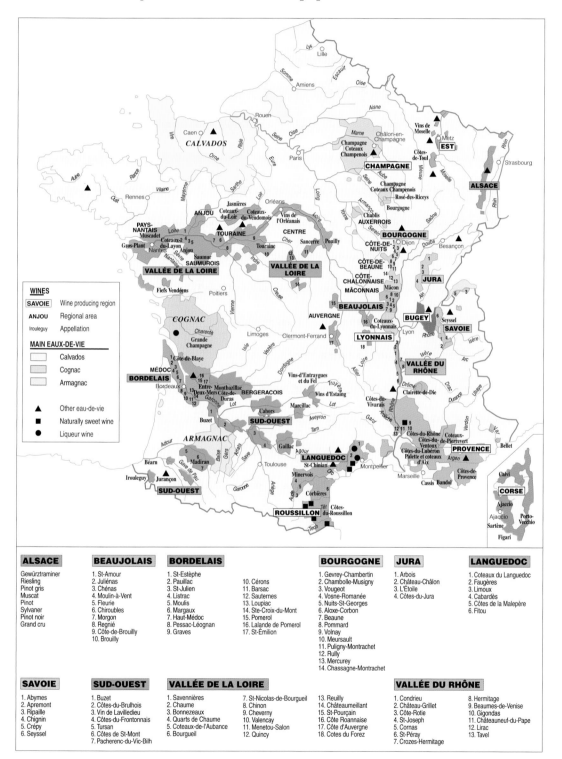

WINES

SAVOIE	Wine producing region
ANJOU	Regional area
Irouleguy	Appellation

MAIN EAUX-DE-VIE

- Calvados
- Cognac
- Armagnac

▲ Other eau-de-vie
■ Naturally sweet wine
● Liqueur wine

ALSACE
Gewürztraminer
Riesling
Pinot gris
Muscat
Pinot
Sylvaner
Pinot noir
Grand cru

BEAUJOLAIS
1. St-Amour
2. Juliénas
3. Chénas
4. Moulin-à-Vent
5. Fleurie
6. Chiroubles
7. Morgon
8. Regnié
9. Côte-de-Brouilly
10. Brouilly

BORDELAIS
1. St-Estèphe
2. Pauillac
3. St-Julien
4. Listrac
5. Moulis
6. Margaux
7. Haut-Médoc
8. Pessac-Léognan
9. Graves
10. Cérons
11. Barsac
12. Sauternes
13. Loupiac
14. Ste-Croix-du-Mont
15. Pomerol
16. Lalande de Pomerol
17. St-Émilion

BOURGOGNE
1. Gevrey-Chambertin
2. Chambolle-Musigny
3. Vougeot
4. Vosne-Romanée
5. Nuits-St-Georges
6. Aloxe-Corton
7. Beaune
8. Pommard
9. Volnay
10. Meursault
11. Puligny-Montrachet
12. Rully
13. Mercurey
14. Chassagne-Montrachet

JURA
1. Arbois
2. Château-Châlon
3. L'Étoile
4. Côtes-du-Jura

LANGUEDOC
1. Coteaux du Languedoc
2. Faugères
3. Limoux
4. Cabardès
5. Côtes de la Malepère
6. Fitou

SAVOIE
1. Abymes
2. Apremont
3. Ripaille
4. Chignin
5. Crépy
6. Seyssel

SUD-OUEST
1. Buzet
2. Côtes-du-Brulhois
3. Vin de Lavilledieu
4. Côtes-du-Frontonnais
5. Tursan
6. Côtes de St-Mont
7. Pacherenc-du-Vic-Bilh

VALLÉE DE LA LOIRE
1. Savennières
2. Chaume
3. Bonnezeaux
4. Quarts de Chaume
5. Coteaux-de-l'Aubance
6. Bourgueil
7. St-Nicolas-de-Bourgueil
8. Chinon
9. Cheverny
10. Valençay
11. Menetou-Salon
12. Quincy
13. Reuilly
14. Châteaumeillant
15. St-Pourçain
16. Côte Roannaise
17. Côte d'Auvergne
18. Cotes du Forez

VALLÉE DU RHÔNE
1. Condrieu
2. Château-Grillet
3. Côte-Rotie
4. St-Joseph
5. Cornas
6. St-Péray
7. Crozes-Hermitage
8. Hermitage
9. Beaumes-de-Venise
10. Gigondas
11. Châteauneuf-du-Pape
12. Lirac
13. Tavel

The **Carnac** Alignments
(megalithic). (Morbihan.)

Rupestrine paintings in the
Font-de-Gaume grotto
(10,000 – 15,000 B.C).
(Dordogne.)

History
and Architecture

35000–10000
The appearance of Homo sapiens. The **Dordogne and Vézère valleys**: rock paintings.

4500–2000
Megalithic civilisation starts to appear in **Brittany,** and **Corsica.**

59–51 B.C.
Gaul, then inhabited by people of Celtic and Iberian origin, is conquered by Julius Cesar. Monuments of great architectural interest have been left by this Gallo-Roman civilisation. During the 3rd century barbarian invasions devastated the country.

481–511
Clovis, King of the Francs was baptised, in 498, at **Reims**.

800
The coronation of Charlemagne, who established a huge western empire. This empire was divided up into three parts by the treaty of Verdun in 843. Western Francie, to the west of the Escaut, Meuse and Rhône rivers, becoming France.

987
Hugues Capet ascends the throne of France.

The Château Comtal c
Carcassonne, a jewel
of medieval military
architecture. (Aude.)

The " Maison Carrée " at **Nîmes**, Roman temple
built during the reign of Auguste. (Gard.)

The chapter of the **Abbey at Fontenay**: asceticism, work and spirituality, the very principles of the monastic life. (Côte-d'Or.)

From the 11th century to the middle of the 12th century

Central power weakness results in a feudal system: local nobility construct fortified castles. The revival of the Christian faith is manifested by the spread of churches, monasteries, and priories. Simplicity of shape, and harmony of space, animated by sculpture which was both innovative and controlled, characterising Roman art.

Vézelay: chapiter of the mystical Mill, an alliance of movement and ease of flow, beginning of the 12th century. (Yonne.)

Middle of the 12th–13th century

Population growth, the development of cities, the enhancement of land, along with the thirst for knowledge raises medieval civilisation to its peak. During this time of enrichment daring cathedrals arose from the ground, particularly in the Greater Paris Area. The use of intersecting ribs in construction reduced the supporting role of walls: masses of light now penetrating through huge stained glass windows.

1337–1475

The One Hundred Years War, within an environment of misery and troubles has the Capetians attempting to repulse the English. Du Guesclin re-establishes order, and in 1429 Joan of Arc liberates Orléans. The treaty of Picquigny (1475), signed by Louis XI, puts an end to hostilities.

Rouen Cathedral nave and choir, an audacious masterpiece of Middle Age period building. (Seine-Maritime.)

16th century

Despite the religious crisis of the Reformation, a wind of renewal blows throughout France: the Renaissance results in the flowering of humanism, and a refined art of living, symbolised by the châteaux of the Loire.

Azay-le-Rideau, one of the most elegant of the Loire châteaux, built between 1518 and 1527. (Indre-et-Loire.)

The Château at **Versailles**: a symbol of the absolute power of royalty during the time of Louis 14th. (Yvelines.)

1643–1715

The reign of Louis XIV, the "Sun King", is a period of military success (France is the major European power), literature (Molière, Racine, Boileau, La Fontaine) and the arts (Mansart, Le Brun). The Château de Versailles reflecting the triumph of absolutism as a synthesis of national resources around an absolute monarchy. This classical architecture (methodical distribution of mass), the expression of controlled passion, is succeeded by baroque which loosens the rules (spanning of volumes, the liberation of symmetry, curves, sculpture). The end of the 18th century is marked by a return to academicism: neo-classical architecture combining new techniques to the magnificence of Greek and Roman antiquity.

1789–1793

An extended political, social, and financial crisis puts an end to the "Ancien Régime". Louis XVI is beheaded on January 21, 1793.

1804–1815

Napoléon is crowned emperor of the French in **Paris**, and perfects France's administrative organisation. But wars with European countries resulting in the abdication at Fontainebleau, and the Waterloo defeat, weaken the country.

1815–1848

After the restoration of the monarchy (Louis XVIII and Charles X), Louis-Philippe establishes a constitutional monarchy prior to being overthrown in February 1848.

Cathedra of the **Church of Conflans-Albertville**: the exuberance of baroque sculpture. (Savoie.)

The neo-classical facade, so called "Louis 16th " of the **Château at Valençay**. (Indre.)

The Viaduc at Garabit, *built between 1882 and 1884 by Gustave Eiffel, has a central span of 116 meters. (Cantal.)*

1848-1870

The Second Republic in 1851 gives way to the Second Empire. The reign of Napoleon III was noted for an expansion of the industrial revolution which was made possible by the development of mechanisation and the use of coal and iron. The disastrous war against Prussia resulted in 1871 in the loss of Alsace, and a part of Lorraine.

The **Orsay Railway Station**, *converted into a museum, built at the end of the 19th century: new techniques enabled increasingly vast buildings to be raised. (Paris.)*

1871-1939

The Third Republic introduced considerable reforms: free and compulsory primary education, trade union legalisation, the separation of Church and State. Foreign policy was oriented towards colonial expansion. The Great War (1914-1918) finished with victory over Germany, but left France worn out. New needs (large department stores, railway stations, exhibition halls) along with revolutionary structures (metal frame structures) gave birth to an architecture oriented towards the liberation of useful surface space, and increasingly larger areas.

The François Mitterrand "Bibliothèque de France": *the use of new materials permits the most daring of shapes. (Paris.)*

1939-1945

The Second World War.

1945 until today

Modernisation of the country, and European construction are the priorities of the Fourth and Fifth Republics. The use of new materials (concrete, aluminium, glass) increases the creativeness of architects.

Alsace

The Alsace region covers of the western slopes of the Vosges and the Rhineland plain which extends from Sundgau in the south to the German border in the north. On the lower slopes of the Vosges thrive the vineyards which for the most part produce the famous Riesling, Sylvaner, and Gewurztraminer white wines. The plain, or ried as it is known, is the area of orchards and grassland. Very picturesque floral villages (Ribeauvillé, Riquewihr, Kayersberg...), consisting of beamed houses are, at times, overlooked by fortified castles.

Strasbourg, Headquarters of the Council of Europe and the European Parliament continues to assert its European prominence at an artistic, intellectual, and political level. Its cathedral, the building of which commenced in 1176, is in pink sandstone from the Vosges, and has a superb radiating facade.

Colmar, at the heart of the Alsace plain, based its prosperity on the wine trade as from the 13th century. The old city charms by its beamed residences, and numerous canals evocative of a "Small Venice".

*The area of **"Petite France" at Strasbourg** is the old tanning and milling quarter. Its houses dating from the Renaissance line the branches of the River Ill. (Bas-Rhin.)*

The red sandstone houses of Riquewihr *form an homogeneous village in the middle of an Alsace vineyard. (Haut-Rhin.)*

The **Haut-Koenigsbourg château** *dominates the plain of Alsace. Its ruins were re-erected at the start of the 20th century by Emperor William II. (Vosges.)*

Further to the south is the lively city of **Mulhouse,** heir to a powerful industrial tradition of which several museums give witness: the National Automobile Museum (the Schlumpf collection), the French Railway Museum, Electropolis, The Printed Fabrics' Museum, and the Wallpaper Museum.

The **Roman church at Murbach,** *near Mulhouse, has retained its flat chevet overlooked by the high towers of the transept. (Haut-Rhin.)*

The **Retable at Buhl** *(about 1500) was painted, probably, for Saint Catherine's convent at Colmar. It depicts scenes from the Passion of Christ. (Haut-Rhin.)*

Aquitaine

The Aquitaine region which combines the Périgord, the Bordeaux region, the Landes area, the Basque Country, and the west of the Pyrenean chain, contains a huge variety of countryside. The Périgord, area, one of the cradles of humanity with its numerous upper Paleolithic (35000 to 10000 B.C) decorated grottoes, is renowned for its conserves, foie gras, and the truffles which form beneath the oak and hazelnut trees which make up the magnificent forests. **Sarlat-la-Canéda**, the capital of Périgord Noir, is proud of its beautiful residences, which date from the 13th century, and were raised by wealthy traders, the middle classes, and magistrates. The Saint-Front cathedral, at **Périgueux**, is the most beautiful example of a Périgord domed church.

**The mellow reliefs
of the "Pays de Cize",**
*in the Basque country, bear the
stamp of the work of man.
(Pyrénées-Atlantiques.)*

The Bordeaux area is universally known for the quality of its vineyards which run along the banks of the Garonne and Gironde rivers. Trade in their produce was for a long time responsible for the prosperity of Bordeaux, first ranking port in the Kingdom during the 15th century, the period during which the Place de la Bourse and the Place du Parlement were built. The Landes' region is one huge forest of pines planted during the last century, on one side bordered by the Atlantic, the surfers paradise. To the south lies the Basque Country a region of noted character which has its own culture, and language. The coast with its ragged cliffs and fine beaches is overlooked by green valleys dotted with white houses, this is the area of Labourd. **Biarritz** is an old fishing port which was transformed during the last century into a seaside resort. The other major resort, **Saint-Jean-de-Luz**, has retained its fishing port which concentrates on sardines, tuna, and anchovies. The ancient provinces of Lower Navarre and Soule present a rugged relief, covered with vast forests of pine and beech. **Pau**, birthplace of Henri IV offers a superb view of the Pyrenees.

Atlantic rains feed the rich **grassland of the Basque country,** *a region devoted to pastoral activity. (Pyrénées-Atlantiques.)*

The church at Oloron-Sainte-Marie *has a Roman portal the arches of which depict the Aged of the Apocalypse, some of them playing music. (Pyrénées-Atlantiques.)*

Old Bordeaux *is one of the most beautiful examples of 18th century town planning. The "Place de la Bourse", designed by the father and son architects, Gabriel, gives witness to the wealth of the city, at that time first ranking port in the Kingdom. (Gironde.)*

The Vineyards of Bordeaux *cover more than 130,000 hectares. Approximately eight thousand "châteaux" produce vintage wines the names of which are a veritable list of fame: Saint-Estèphe, Margaux, Pauillac, Château-Yquem, Saint-Emilion... (Gironde.)* Ph. R. Nourry

Aquitaine

The Landes' Forest *was first planted in the 19th century. It consists of maritime pines, a fast growing rectilinear tree. (Landes.)*
The large beach *at Saint-Jean-de-Luz, between the Pyrenees and the Atlantic Ocean. (Pyrénées-Atlantiques.)*

Bayonne, between "les Landes" and the Basque country, *is the economic centre of the Adour region. The banks of the River Nive are lined with big picturesque houses. (Pyrénées-Atlantiques.)*

The Roque-Gageac is considered to be the most beautiful site in the Dordogne valley. Its houses with roofs or flag stones and tiles are bunched together at the bottom of the cliff. (Dordogne.)

Périgueux was for a long time shared between the City, once part of ancient Vésone, and the powerful monastic centre of Puy-Saint-Front which attracted a multitude of pilgrims. (Dordogne.)

The Walled town of Monpazier, *founded by Edward 1st, Duke of Aquitaine and King of England, was part of the system of defence established in the Périgord as from 1267. (Dordogne.)*

The Fortress at Bonaguil *(15th-16th centuries) is a fine example of architecture which integrated firearms within its defensive system. (Lot-et-Garonne.)*

Auvergne

The volcanic massifs of the Auvergne form the backbone of the Massif Central which covers a major part of the region. From the south to the north, the Cantal (highest point being the Plomb du Cantal 1,858 meters) the heights of Dore (Puy de Sancy, 1,886 meters) and Dome (Puy de Dome, 1,463 meters) – puy signifying mountain in auvergnat- make for original scenery consisting of cones, more or less eroded, and lakes the result of certain valleys being closed by the flow of lava; On the slopes forests and pasture alternate, and provide grazing for the tough tan coated salers cattle. Numerous mineral

The Sancy volcanic massif
is a paradise for strolling enthusiasts; its numerous paths criss-cross a preserved environment. (Puy-de-Dôme.)

AUVERGNE

and hot water springs have resulted in the founding of a considerable number of medical treatment spas. To the east of these volcanoes the Bourbonnais mountains, the Forez and Livradois, alternate with pasture and forests.

At the foot of the Puy-de-Dôme lies **Clermont-Ferrand** which is partially built from stone formed from lava. Since the end of the last century it has become the city of the tyre, and Headquarters of the Michelin company. Moulins, the Bourbonnais capital has numerous agricultural connected activities: food produce, foot wear .... Aurillac, at the centre of Upper Auvergne has retained and old area of winding narrow streets which descend to the Jordanne river. The Puy-en-Velay occupies an original location in a huge basin bristling with volcanic needles, on one of these the cathedral of Notre-Dame has been raised .

The Auvergne Volcano Park,
*to the west of Clermont-Ferrand,
is a real open air museum
of volcanic shapes. (Puy-de-Dôme.)*

Thiers *has, for several centuries now,
specialised in cutlery. The Museum of Cutlery:
knife with carved ivory handle.
(Puy-de-Dôme.)*

The Church of Saint-Nectaire *raised in a verdant environment, is a fine example of Auvergne Roman architecture. Its chevet has an elegant disposition. (Puy-de-Dôme.)*

The Basilica of Saint Julien de Brioude *is the biggest Roman building in the Auvergne area. The warm colouring emanating from the red sandstone and a fine polychrome paving characterise the nave, the first spans of which are supported by grouped pillars of engaged columns. (Haute-Loire.)*

The Cantal *consists of a volcanic relief ground down by glaciers where forest and rich pasture land alternate. (Cantal.)*

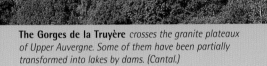

The Gorges de la Truyère *crosses the granite plateaux of Upper Auvergne. Some of them have been partially transformed into lakes by dams. (Cantal.)*

Aurillac, *at the crossroads of the Upper Auvergne tourist routes, has retained its old quarter on the banks of the River Jordanne. (Cantal.)*

Burgundy

Beaune, capital of the Burgundy rich patrimony vineyard, *is proud of its general hospital which was founded in 1143 along Flemish lines, for the accommodation of the sick and afflicted. Its roofs are covered with glazed tiles. (Côte-d'Or.)*

Burgundy owes its fame to a rich historical past, the dynasty of the Grand Dukes of Valois (1364-1477), and to the prestigious "Côte" vines which border the "mountain" that dominates the plain of the Saône river. Ancient capital of the Dukes of Burgundy, **Dijon**, since the 15th century became a wealthy city endowed with remarkable monuments: the Dukes' Palace and Burgundy Assembly, the Church of Notre-Dame, and the Hôtel de Vogüe.

To the west the Massif of Morvan retains huge natural open spaces with scattered habitation. The scenery is dominated by forests on the high ground, and hedged pasture land on the slopes. **Nevers**, washed by the Loire river, is famous for its glazed earthenware which was introduced around 1565 by artists of Italian origin. From Auxerre to Dijon stretches the extended Burgundy limestone plateau, which is crossed by numerous rivers and canals which are used for river tourism

Auxerre, the capital of Lower Burgundy, is on the banks of the River Yonne, its old quarter dominated by the Saint-Etienne Cathedral. To the south, hills and undulating plateaux make up the Charollais country, the rich pasture land which is used for raising the reputed beef cattle. The Saône valley, passage way to the south of France, enjoys considerable economic activity which is especially noticeable around **Chalon-sur-Saône**.

The vitality of Roman art is to be seen everywhere; the finest examples being at **Cluny**, **Paray-le-Monial**, **Autun**, **Saulieu** and **Vézelay**.

Cluny Abbey, *founded during the 10th century, is where the extraordinary influence of the Benedictines throughout the Europe of the Middle Ages originated. Very fine capitals originating from the church are exhibited in the flour store. (Saône-et-Loire.)*

*Between Chagny and Dijon, to the south of Beaune, the **Burgundian vineyard** disposes of 37,500 hectares on the slopes which produce the most famous, prestigiously named, vintages in the world: Gevrey-Chambertin, Clos-Vougeot, Vosne-Romanée, Nuits-Saint-Georges, Aloxe-Corton, Pommard. Above: the cellars of the Meursault estate. To the right: grape harvesting on the "Hautes-Côtes de Beaune". (Côte-d'Or.)*

The Fontenay Abbey, *founded in 1118, is built in the architectural tradition of the Cistercians; a visit to the buildings (here the cloister) gives an appreciation of the day in the life of a monk. (Côte-d'Or.)*

The estate of the Clos-Vougeot Château *belongs to the Tastevin (wine tasting) Fraternity who meet each year in chapter to enthrone new members. The order works for the promotion of the wines of both Burgundy and France as a whole. (Côte-d'Or.)*

The Philippe-le-Bon tower which dominates the Dukes' Palace and the Burgundy Assembly, the view takes in the greater part of Dijon. **The Hôtel de Vogüe**, *covered with glazed tiles, adjoins the elegant gothic construction of* **the church of Notre-Dame**. *(Côte-d'Or.)*

The Bussy-Rabutin Château, *an ancient fortress transformed during the 16th century by Antoine de Chandio into a hospitable residence, on his return from Italy, owes its fame to its interior decoration. This was done by Roger de Rabutin, exiled in Burgundy for having sang songs which made light of the relationship of Louis XIV and Marie Mancini, allegorical panels can be admired along with portraits of famous gentlemen and ladies of the court. (Côte-d'Or.)*

Brittany

Brittany firstly brings to mind the coastline "Armor", of which 1,300 kilometres include an infinity of points, coves, and creeks which shelter the fishing ports of **Brest, Lorient**, Le Guilvinec, **Concarneau, Douarnenez**, and **Paimpol**, and a string of isles exposed to the onslaughts of the ocean: Bréhat, Ouessant, Sein, Groix, and Belle-Ile. The interior of the country "Argoat" is partially covered with forests and moors, retaining much evidence of its still living faith in its granite sculpted enclosures and wayside crosses. Agriculture along with the raising of stock occupy a very important place in the local economy: early fruit and vegetables, pork, poultry, and dairy products are exported throughout the entire world.

*To the west of Cape Fréhel lies **Erquy** which is devoted to coastal fishing, mainly for scallops. Its beaches are sheltered from the wind and the ocean swell. (Côtes-d'Armor.)*

The Raz Point *is located at the end of Cape Sizun. It's sombre rocky bulk surrounds, along with Sein island, the very dangerous Raz de Sein with its violent currents and scattering of reefs. (Finistère.)*

Ancient capital of the Duchy of Brittany, then administrative centre of the province when it became part of France as a result of the marriage of Anne de Bretagne to Charles VIII in 1491, **Rennes**, during the last few decades has experienced considerable development in the fields of electronics, telecommunications, and data processing. Its universities have almost 40,000 students.

Vannes, beside the Gulf of Morbihan, retains behind its ramparts picturesque old quarters, and its small port is a point of departure for boat trips. At the mouth of the Odet Estuary, **Quimper**, the ancient capital of Cornwall, is the city which remains the most Breton of the region. Its narrow lanes running from old houses lead to the Cathedral of Saint-Corentin.

Saint-Brieuc, close to the sea, is primarily an administrative and commercial centre, the exhibitions and markets of which have an influence on the entire department.

The Pink Granite Coast *is like a stack of oddly shaped rocks. by following the "chemin des douaniers", the stroller attempts to find, in all this chaos of granite, the "rabbit", the "tortoise", and the "mushroom"... (Côtes-d'Armor.)*

Saint-Malo *as from the 16th century, ensured its prosperity by taking part in the Canadian fur trade, and fishing for cod in the waters off Newfoundland. Ferries connect it with the south of England. (Ille-et-Vilaine.)*

The head-dress *makes for the originality of the traditional Breton costume. The Bigouden head-dress is that of a high cylindrical lace, and is without doubt the most original. (Finistère.)*

The granite rocks of Huelgoat *are one of the strangest sites in inland Brittany. They form, along with the neighbouring forest, a much visited excursion centre with evocative names: the Devil's Grotto, the Chaos of the Mill... (Finistère.)*

The jube of the Saint-Fiacre-du-Faouët Chapel
*is a masterpiece of high polychrome wood art.
(Morbihan.)*

The Brasparts Calvary,
*in the heart of the Arrée
Mountains possesses one
of the most moving pieta
in Brittany. (Finistère.)*

Centre

The Central region of France, also known as the Centre-Val de Loire, is located at the heart of France, a bridge between regions as distant from each other as Normandy and the Auvergne, the Limousin and the Greater Paris Area. To the

The château at Villandry *is famous for its gardens, including the varied coloured seasonal vegetable patch, the result of medieval monastic gardens. It is completely renewed twice per annum. (Indre-et-Loire.)*

north the Eure-et-Loire countryside is dominated by extended areas of cereal cultivation which have something in common with the Paris Basin. **Chartres**, as a result of the spires of its cathedral, is visible from a long distance across this immense sea of wheat. The cathedral's sculptured decor consists of 4,000 figures, and its collection of stained-glass windows depicts 5,000 individuals.

Chambord, *built by François 1st from 1519 onwards is the largest of the Loire chateaux. Of perfect architectural consistency it has 440 rooms accessed by 83 staircases. (Loir-et-Cher.)*

The Indre-et-Loire, the Loir-et-Cher and the Loiret are washed by the Loire, the longest river in France. On its course **Tours** (the cathedral of Saint-Gatien), the major Loire valley city. **Blois**, the château of which is located in the city centre and was designed by Louis XIIth, François 1st and Gaston d'Orléans, and **Orléans** (Sainte-Croix cathedral), the capital of medieval France.

The Indre and the Cher Departments, to the south make up the Berry, one of the oldest agricultural regions of France. This is a slightly raised, extensive, and highly fertile plateau, to the south of which is hill country. To the east, the Sancerrois area is famous for its vines which flourish on banks of chalk.

The old quarters of **Bourges**, and its cathedral, at the heart of the Champagne Berry area remind one of its rich medieval past. During the 12th century the city was an archbishopric, an advanced post of the Kingdom faced with the territories of the South West dominated by the inhabitants of Anjou. **Châteauroux**, a communications crossroads, is an active industrial city (mechanics, farm produce) which retains a medieval part of town.

Since the north wing was demolished in during the 18th century, the courtyard of the **Château de Chaumont** *overlooks the Loire River. It was one this spot that Henry II Plantagenêt had his last meeting with Thomas Becket before this last was murdered at Canterbury. (Loir-et-Cher.)*

The modest hamlet of Nohant *has an elegant 18th century residence, made famous by its owner George Sand (1804-1876), who had as guests Chopin, Delacroix, Liszt... (Indre.)*

The Notre-Dame-de-la-Belle-Verrière *is one of the most precious of the stained glass windows in Chartres Cathedral: the radiant blue of the central panels (12th century) enhances the more intense blues used by the 13th century master. (Eure-et-Loire.)*

Bourges, Saint-Etienne Cathedral *(1200-1270): the visitor can, if located at the end of the building, between the last two pillars, be profoundly affected by the formidable vertical impulse of the choir, the vaults of which are 37 meters from the ground. (Cher.)*

The Saint-Gatien Cathedral at Tours *has a remarkable flamboyant facade: festoon archivolts, ornamental leaf gables. (Indre-et-Loire.)*

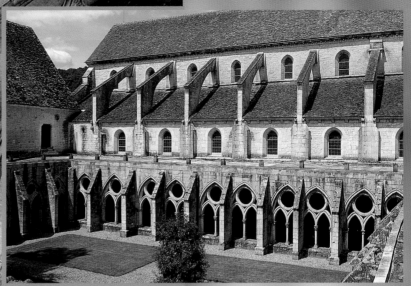

The Noirlac Benedictine Abbey, *in the Cher Valley, remains the most complete and best preserved monastic setting in France. The, end of 13th century, multifoiled, gothic cloister has fine small columns, the capitals of which are decorated with plants. (Cher.)*

Founded in 650, **the abbey of Saint-Benoît-sur-Loire** *was destroyed during the French Revolution. All that remains is the remarkable abbey church preceded by a huge 9th century tower porch of Carthaginian influence. (Loiret.)*

Champagne-Ardenne

At the heart of the Champagne area, on the slopes of the Marne valley and to the south of Epernay, flourishes the famous Champagne wine growing area which exports its production throughout the entire world. **Reims**, the city of coronations, owes its fame to two major monuments: the Roman basilica of Saint-Remi, and the Gothic cathedral, the facade of which is one of the most beautiful in France. The city contains numerous Champagne cellars, which are open to the public. From **Châlons-en-Champagne** to **Troyes** stretches a huge plain (chalky Champagne), devoted to the large scale agricultural production of cereals and beets. Châlons, crossed by the the Mau and Nau canals which originate in the Marne river, has very pretty 17th and 18th century hotels, and timber frame houses. The ancient capital of Champagne, Troyes has preserved a beautiful old quarter with numerous churches, along with a cathedral of impressive dimensions.

Towards the east and south the countryside becomes more irregular around Bar-sur-Aube and Bar-sur-Seine, then the immense Langres' plateau appears. Being at the junction of several roads, **Chaumont** has played an active commercial role since the Middle Ages.

The small wine producing market town of Hautvilliers, *in the heart of the Champagne wine area, has elegant wrought iron signs. (Marne.)*

The Castellane Champagne cellars *at Epernay, extend over 10 kilometres. A museum devoted to the Champagne Tradition enables the work of cellarmen and coopers to be discovered. (Marne.)*

Troyes Cathedral *is a major work of Champagne gothic, undertaken in 1208. The nave is a remarkable three floor erection, of total openwork design. (Aube.)*

The Ardennes, to the north, are a primary massif covered with forests and crossed by the meandering Meuse river. Charleville-Mézières, the administrative and commercial city, has not forgotten the poet Arthur Rimbaud.

The Notre-Dame-en-Vaux cloister's museum, *at Châlons-en-Champagne, exhibits 12th century sculptures which decorated a cloister which was discovered in 1960. (Marne.)*

The statue of the Ange au sourire *(Smiling Angel) on the facade of* **Reims** *Cathedral, reveals a Champagne style of architecture characterised by visual vivacity, and liberty of attitude. (Marne.)*

Corsica

Corsica is the highest of the Mediterranean islands, reaching 2,706 meters at its highest point at the Monte Cinto. Its 1,000 km of rocky coast are deeply indented, alternating between deep gulfs, small creeks, and tapering headlands. In the interior, the mountains and high valleys are sprinkled with picturesque perched villages.

Bastia, to the north of the island, was, throughout the occupation by Genoa during the war of independence (1729-1769) towards the end of the 14th century, the administrative and financial capital of Corsica. The city developed on each side of the old port, the large houses which are at the bottom of the mountain composing an attractive scene.

The archeological site at Filitosa has prehistoric remains which contain a wealth of information regarding this period of history: the menhir statues were carved about 1500 B.C. by the Toréens, a sea going people who settled the land.

Ajaccio is an ancient Genoese colony situated in the hollow of a superb gulf. The city experienced considerable development during the 18th century, and is the place where Napoléon Bonaparte was born in 1769.

The church of San Michele at Murato (1280) is a fine example of pisan Roman art. It is recognisable by its polychromic bonding of alternating white limestone moellons, and dark green serpentine. (Haute-Corse.)

The **Filitosa** menhirs statues. (Corse-du-Sud.)

The Gulf of Porto and the Scandola natural reserve *with their pink granite cliffs plunging vertically into the blue sea are the most spectacular natural sites in Corsica. (Corse-du-Sud.)*

Saint-Florent and its marina *are superbly located in the hollow of a very beautiful gulf. (Corse-du-Sud.)*

Franche-Comté

The Franche-Comté consists of three distinct entities. To the east, the mountains and the high plateaux of the Jura form a crescent oriented from the south towards the north east, an alternation of dark fir tree forests, and extensive pastures. Water is to be seen everywhere, in the form of torrents, water falls, springs, and resurgences. The freshness and beauty of the scenery has been praised by numerous poets, i.e. Ruskin, the Englishman, Goethe the German, and Lamartine, French. To the west, a huge plateau, crossed by the Saône river, is demarcated to the north by the rounded tops of the Vosges covered with superb forests.

The Franche-Comté is reputed for its production of dairy products, pride of place going to the comté, a gruyère type cheese which has matured in cellars known as fruitières for between six to eight months.

Besançon has an original location in the middle of a loop in the Doubs river, overlooked by steep hills the strategic importance of which did not go unnoticed by Cesar. Vauban, on the order of Louis XIV, had a formidable stronghold built, which can still be visited today. Besançon is the French capital of the clock and watch making industry.

The **Belfort** Gap, accessed by the railway, motorway, and the Rhône-Rhine canal, links the Rhenish country and, beyond that of the Franche-Comté, and the south of France. Since time immemorial this has been the route of the invader.

The High Plateaux of the Jura *is an ideal spot to practice cross country skiing. The Great Jura Crossing – Grande Traversée du Jura (GTJ)—is marked out over 250 kilometres. (Doubs, Jura.)*

The old royal salt works at Arc-et-Senans *is one of the last example of end of 18th century industrial architecture. This "ideal" city was designed by Claude-Nicolas Ledoux. (Doubs.)*

RÉGION DE FRANCHE-COMTÉ

The Château at Joux
dominates the Pontarlier
valley, an access used since
time immemorial. It was built
during the 11 century by the
Joux nobility who levied a toll
for right of way. (Doubs.)

**The bell of the Church of
Rochejean** is typical of the
Franche-Comté style, with its
contours and glazed tiles.
(Doubs).

The Greater Paris Area

Ever since the Capetians made it their capital in the 12th century, Paris has seen the erection of numerous prestigious monuments, which give witness to its economic and political importance. The cathedral of Notre Dame on the Ile de la Cité, with its wonderful proportional equilibrium is one of the finest examples of French gothic in existence. The Champs-Elysées, lined by the head offices of major companies, and luxury shopping, runs from the Place de la Concorde to the Arc de Triomphe which was raised on the orders of Napoléon. The Eiffel Tower, built to commemorate the Universal Exhibition of 1889, is one of the masterpieces of metal construction, a combination of lightness of form ,and strength. Montmartre, dominated by the church of the Sacré-Cœur, during the last century, and until 1914, was the favourite part of town for authors and artists. Political power resides in the Elysée Palace (the President of the Republic), at the Palais-Bourbon (the National Assembly), and the Luxembourg Palais (the Senat).

The Pont Neuf, *the oldest bridge in Paris, was the first to have sidewalks. It consists of two bridges separated by a statue of Henry IV. (Paris.)*

The Cathedral of Notre-Dame *was built between 1163 and 1345, the wonderful equilibrium of its proportions makes it one of the most beautiful of French gothic examples. (Paris.)*

With its railway stations and airports, Paris is an international communications crossroads where the High Speed Rail Network, and numerous motorways converge.

The châteaux, parks, and cathedrals of the Greater Paris Area are also evocative of a rich historical past. The château at Versailles being representative of the absolute power of royalty during the reign of Louis XIV. The château at Fontainebleau has been converted, and lived in, by every French sovereign from the 13th century to Napoléon III, whilst the basilica of Saint-Denis contains the tombs of almost all the Kings of France, from Dagobert to Louis XVIII.

A surround of forests and magnificent valleys (Seine, Oise, Marne) give this region, which has seen the development of numerous new towns, a certain appeal.

Crowning the hill of Montmartre, the **Sacré-Cœur** *was built after the defeat of 1870. It is a pastiche of Byzantine art. (Paris.)*

The Place de la Concorde has for centrepiece one of the Luxor obelisks which was offered to France by the viceroy of Egypt Mehemet-Ali during the visit of Jean-François Champollion, in 1829. The Place was arranged by Gabriel from 1755 to 1775. Two hotels with beautiful colonnades line the rue Royale. (Paris.)

From the top of the Eiffel Tower Paris and its monuments are overlooked:
here, the Grand Palais, the Place de la Concorde, the church of La Madeleine, and the Opera. In the foreground the bridges of les Invalides and that of Alexander III. (Paris.)

The Mirror Room at the Château at Versailles *is one huge 75 meter long reception room. Seventeen large windows give out onto the park with their seventeen panels comprising 578 mirrors. This gallery was used for major court ceremonies and celebrations. Proclamation of the German Empire was made their on January 18th 1871, and the treaty of Versailles signed on June 28, 1919. (Yvelines.)*

The château of Vaux-le-Vicomte *is one of the most beautiful successes of 17th century classical architecture. It was raised by Louis Le Vau for Nicolas Fouquet, Lord High Treasurer to Louis XIV. The monument is an integral part of a huge landscaped assembly designed by Le Nôtre, including paths, ornamental ponds, and statues. (Seine-et-Marne.)*

The Louvre, a onetime palace of French kings, *it was made into a museum during the 18th century with the opening to the public of the "Grande Galerie". The main entrance is via the pyramid in glass designed by I. M. Pei. The six departments of the museum deal with all major artistic periods from Antiquity to the 19th century (Paris.)*

The first large department stores *were built at the end of the 19th century: Printemps and the Galeries Lafayette having huge halls lit by glass roofs supported by metal frames. (Paris.)*

The area of **La Défense** at the gates of Paris, is a business area comprising tower blocks arranged around a vast open space. Escalators lead to the "Grande Arche" where there is a fine outlook onto the La Défense development, with on the left the CNIT which consists of 80,000 square meters of covered surface area. (Hauts-de-Seine.)

The Georges Pompidou Centre (National Centre for Art and Culture) was designed by the architects Rogers and Piano who used steel framework, and partitions in glass. Here can be found a public information library, the Centre for Industrial Creation, the Institute for Research and Acoustics' Co-ordination (IRCAM), and the National Museum of Modern Art. (Paris.)

Languedoc-Roussillon

The vast Languedoc-Roussillon region is a collection of a great variety of landscapes, from the high plateaux of the Aubrac Lozère, to the rugged banks of the Côte Vermeille. To the north the Gorges du Tarn deeply gouges the extensive sheep grazed limestone plateaux. Grottoes and chasms are evidence of the slow wear of running water. The Cévennes range of mountains appear like a series of heavy granite summits covered with a dark mantle of forest. More to the south the scenery becomes Mediterranean, and the vine is increasingly to be seen

The Benedictine abbey of Saint-Martin-du-Canigou
is located at a site the altitude of which is 1,094 meters. The buildings, which were constructed during the 11th century, have three cloister galleries remaining (the fourth, which opens out onto the mountain, has been restored), and the church with its massive keep like steeple. (Pyrénées-Orientales.)

on the mellow slopes of the Hérault and the Aude Valley. Lastly, the Corbières area, an immense patchwork of orchards and vineyards, and the Fenouillèdes give way to the Roussillon overlooked by the heights of the Pyrenees.

Located in the narrow threshold which separates the Massif Central from the Pyrenees, the prosperity of the fortified city of **Carcassonne** is based on the wine trade. **Perpignan**, the principle city of the Roussillon, with its warm and vivacious atmosphere is evocative of nearby Catalonia. **Montpellier**, for a long time, had profited from the trade in spices with the Eastern Mediterranean prior to becoming, during the reign of Louis XIV, the administrative capital of Lower Languedoc. The old quarter of Montpellier has fine monuments dating from the 17th and 18th centuries. Between Garrigue and the Costière du Gard, **Nîmes** continues to be marked by Gallo-Roman antiquity: one should see the arenas, the Maison Carrée and, a few kilometres to the north east, the Pont du Gard which carries across the Gardon valley an aqueduct which supplies Nîmes with fresh spring water. In the middle of a huge expanse of marshland and lakes, **Aigues-Mortes** was founded by Saint-Louis anxious to possess a stronghold on the Mediterranean coastline.

The Fenouillèdes is hard countryside of average size mountains located between the region of Corbières and Roussillon. Its slopes, covered with scrubland and holm oak, give way at times to the vine. (Pyrénées-Orientales.)

The Palace of the Kings of Majorca *is a reminder of the time when Perpignan, during the 14th and 15th centuries, was the advanced post of Catalan civilisation north of the Pyrenees. Today, it is a commercial, highly vivacious, city the dynamism of which lies partially in the export of fruit and wines produced close by. (Pyrénées-Orientales.)*

Peyrepertuse, *perched on a rocky spur, is the largest of the cathar châteaux. A refuge for the Cathars, it fell after three days of combat in November 1240. Saint Louis made it the main stronghold facing the region of Roussillon. (Aude.)*

The old village of **Saint-Guilhem-le-Désert** *is gathered around the old abbey, at the outlet of wild gorges. The 9th century abbey church has a highly ornate chevet. The apse is crowned by arcades separated by fine small columns. (Hérault.)*

*Located in a tight sill which separates the Massif Central from the Pyrenees, **the city of Carcassonne** controls the route from the Atlantic to the Mediterranean, and between France and Spain. At around 1130, Trencavel nobility built their fortified château.(p. 6). The fortress was annexed by France as a result of the Albigensian Crusade (1224-1226). Louis IX then Philippe le Hardi constructed a second external boundary which made the place practically attack proof. (Aude.)*

__Fontfroide Abbey__ nestles at the hollow of a small Corbières' valley populated with cypress trees and arbutus. In 1093, several monks in search for a place to pray founded this monastery, which, in 1143, became part of the order of Cistercians. In the Middle Ages Fontfroide was to be a bulwark of orthodoxy confronted by Catharism. (Aude.)

It was **the Pont du Gard** which conveyed, across the valley of the River Gardon, 20,000 cubic meters of water, via a 49 kilometre long aqueduct from a spring close to Uzès to Nîmes. Constructed in 19 B.C. by the Romans, it superposes three levels of arcade composed of enormous moellons. (Gard.)

Rising above the middle of a vast area of marshes and lakes, **Aigues-Mortes** was created by Saint Louis, for the purposes of having a stronghold on the Mediterranean coastline along with a place for departure for the crusades. (Gard.)

The Gorges du Tarn *are a deep gash in the extensive limestone plateaux which cover the south east of the Massif Central. The river has used a series of natural rifts to clear a way through. (Lozère.)*

The Fenestrelle Tower *gives witness to the medieval past of Uzès. (Gard.)*

Limousin

Surrounding Limoges the landscape is one of average hills consisting of hedges and grazing land, the home of the Limousin cattle, divided up by copses of oak, beech, and chestnut trees. **Limoges**, the administrative and university city, owes its fame to the manufacture of its porcelain of renown.

To the south east lies the Millavaches plateau a scattering of stony areas exposed to the wind and plentiful rainfall which acts as a source of water for numerous rivers (Creuse, Vienne, Corrèze...). This rough environment explains its very low population. Around **Guéret**, and the Marche, a countryside made up of wooded valleys and grazing, is one of transition from the Val de Loire and The Massif Central. Capital of the Comté de la Marche during the 13th century, Guéret has retained its position as administrative centre, whilst Aubusson owes its prosperity to the clear waters of the River Creuse which encouraged the development of the tanning industry, and later of tapestry-making.

Between the Vézère and Dordogne are the plateaux of the Lower Limousin, the granite soil of which has been gouged by the Corrèze river and above all the Dordogne river descending from the Massif Central. **Brive-la-Gaillarde** is an

Brive-la-Gaillarde *owes its name to the number of sieges it suffered. The Hôtel de Labenche is the most beautiful building in the city. It's style is that of typical Toulouse Renaissance. (Corrèze.)*

Limoges is universally known for its china.
The Adrien-Dubouché museumexhibits more than 10,000 pieces originating from manufacturers throughout the entire world. (Haute-Vienne.)

*Quite close to the Millevaches plateau, **Meymac** has retained intact its old houses which are gathered around the 12th-13th century abbey church. Its chevet is of restrained appearance (Corrèze.)*

active town (canning, food produce), located in the middle of an enormous basin given over to the cultivation of fruit and market garden produce. **Tulle** is situated in an original location on the steep slopes of the Corrèze River, over-looked by the cathedral of Notre-Dame, the remains of a one time abbey.

The Millevaches Plateau (thousand springs)
is the water tower of the Limousin. Its granite heights are moors covered with heather, ferns, and broken up by a few forests. (Corrèze, Creuse.)

The Merle Towers *(13th century) did not resist the arrival of artillery, which, from the heights, could bombard them without difficulty. (Corrèze.)*

The old houses of Turenne *are tightly grouped around the château. The Viscount of Turenne, during the 15th century, had more than 1,200 villages under his control. (Corrèze.)*

The church of the old Abbaye of Moutier-d'Ahun *contains a surprising collection of sculptured panelling and stalls dating from between 1673 and 1683 by Simon Baüer, the artist from Auvergne. (Creuse.)*

Lorraine

The region of the Lorraine consists of plateaux, slightly inclining towards the west, and the eastern slopes of the Jura mountains. To the north these plateaux are broken up by a succession of north south running hilly inclines covered with forests and bottom ground consisting of both grazing and arable land. A frontier region, Lorraine has for a long time been influenced by the hostility of European Nations, as the remains of past battles and fortifications give witness. Struck by the decline in traditional industry (mining, and steel), Lorraine has undergone considerable readjustment characterised by a concern for diversification. **Nancy**, the ancient capital of the Duchy of Lorraine, has retained its remarkable architectural heritage surrounding the Place Stanislas, a perfect example of elegance and equilibrium. **Metz**, for a long time was a religious metropolis, and a first category military establishment. The city is dominated by the Cathedral of Saint-Etienne.

To the south, the mountains of the Vosges are covered with a thick cover of forest which thins out, then disappears above 1,000 meters to become stubble land which is covered with snow during the winter. The plain which extends to the west of the Vosges is especially endowed with hot springs: **Vittel** and **Contrexéville** being two of the most well known spars.

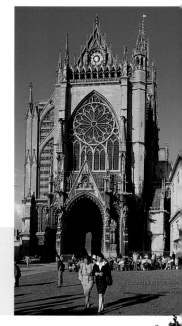

Metz, *the ancient capital of Lotharingie, has always been a religious city and place of utmost military importance being close to the Franco-German border. (Moselle.)*

The Lunéville pottery works, *one time royal manufacturer, produced for the most part china for the table. The finest examples can be admired at the museum located in the château. Here, the "Baby", King Stanislas dwarf. (Meuthe-et-Moselle.)*

*Ancient capital of the Dukes of Lorraine, **Nancy** has retained a remarkable architectural heritage. The Place Stanislas is a perfect example of elegance and equilibrium which was characteristic of the French 18th century. Stanislas Leszczynski, father in law of Louis XV, decided in 1752 to develop an area which was intended to reunite the old quarter of Nancy with the new town. The close co-operation between Emmanuel Héré, the architect, and Jean Lamour, the genius wrought iron craftsman grants the whole a rare harmony. (Meurthe-et-Moselle.)*

The Lorraine slopes of the Vosges mountains
*are covered with a thick covering of forest, and are part
of the Vosges Ballons Regional Park. (Vosges.)*

Midi-Pyrénées

The Midi-Pyrénées join together on both sides of the Garonne river passage, very distinct geographical entities, from the Pyrenees to the south and to the foothills of the Massif Central to the north.

The Pyrenean mountain chain raises its snowy peaks and ragged crests above hanging valleys covered with forests and extended pastures. This is the playground of the rambler and winter sports, and spectacular sites like the amphitheatre at Gavarnie.

Valleys running from north to south demarcate countryside of well defined character: the Bigorre and the Comminges areas are rolling countryside which is dotted with white houses, the Ariège with its cave riddled slopes. **Tarbes**, **Saint-Gaudens** and **Foix** are small flourishing towns where life is good, and form a link between the hard mountain climate, and the milder Gascon countryside. At its centre lie the hills of Armagnac the home of the famous eau-de-vie the distilling process of which requires the greatest of care.

The Garonne countryside, on each side of the river, rises in terraces covered with huge orchards, vines, and cereals. **Toulouse**, with its superb monuments (the Basilica of Saint-Sernin, the Jacobins' cloister) is built in brick, hence its name

The Pyrenees Mountain Chain *extends, over approximately 500 kilometres, from the Atlantic to the Mediterranean. The central portion bristles with granite outcrops such as the Néouvielle massif, formed by glacial erosion. (Hautes-Pyrénées)*

At the heart of the Ariège Department, *the Ancient Château of the Counts of Foix has retained its defensive watch towers. (Ariège.)*

of the "pink city", and is a highly active regional city, famous for aeronautic and aerospace construction.

Further to the north the vines of Albi (**Gaillac** wine) are planted around villages crowned with little knolls. The Grands Causses, vast stony arid limestone plateaux, the home of sheep, cover part of the Aveyron. Finally, Rouergue and Upper Quercy alternate their wooded and limestone plateaux with steep-sided valleys. Numerous caves attract potholing enthusiasts, whilst for those interested in the dawn of humanity (prehistoric engravings, and rock art).

The Midi Peak at Bigorre *stands out above the Pyrenees at 2,865 meters. On the summit is an observatory and scientific research institute. (Hautes-Pyrénées.)*

The Cathedral of Sainte-Marie at Auch, *stalls carved between 1500 and 1552. (Gers.)*

Toulouse owes to brick, the most used material in the construction of its monuments, its other name of the "pink city". The "Place du Capitole" is the favourite meeting place for the people of Toulouse. (Haute-Garonne.)

During the 13th century **Albi** sheltered followers of the Cathar sect who were persecuted by the forces of the Inquisition. Its cathedral, Saint Cécile, started in 1282, has the appearance of a fortress. (Tarn.)

The Abbey at Moissac, *founded during the 7th century, reached its most influential period during the 11th and 12th centuries. It is from this period that the cloister with fine marble columns supporting very varied chapiters dates. (Tarn-et-Garonne.)*

The treasure of the Sainte-Foy-de-Conques church *exhibits the striking 10th century statue and relic of Saint Foy, recovered with gold and precious stones. (Aveyron.)*

Lautrec, *an ancient fortified place with a picturesque maze of little streets lined with old houses, it is famous for its incomparably flavoured pink garlic. (Tarn.)*

The old houses of Estaing, *on the banks of the River Lot, are overlooked by the château which was built between the 15th and 16th centuries. (Lo*

Rocamadour, *with its dwellings, sanctuaries, tourelles and fortified gates sticking to the cliff face, is one of the most visited sites in France. (Lot.)*

The Lot has dug its bed over the Quercy plateaux *and runs between the steep slopes of hard limestone covered with chestnut groves. (Lot.)*

Nord-Pas-de-Calais

The central part of the Pas-de-Calais consists of the Artois hills which separate the flat lands of Lens and Arras from the Boulonnais, a country-side of thickets and whitewashed farms. **Boulogne** remains the first ranking fishing port of France. To the north, is the Côte d'Opale area, cape Blanc-Nez and cape Gris-Nez, which are at the extremity of the limestone plateau from which the tunnel under the English Channel was excavated. **Calais**, located only 38 km from England, is the first ranking port of France for passenger traffic.

The Grand-Place at Arras *is a unique collection of Flemish style 17th and 18th century houses supported by arcades intended to protect market traders and customers from inclement weather. (Pas-de-Calais.)*

Lille takes advantage of its geographical position *to become, at the centre of the North-South axis, one of the large European metropolises. The "Place Général De Gaulle" (Main Square) is the centre of Lille life. (Nord.)*

Boulogne *is the first ranking port in continental Europe for fresh fish, and boats come to berth alongside the Gambetta wharf. (Pas-de-Calais.)*

The Côte d'Opale *between Cape Blanc-Nez and Cape Gris-Nez. (Pas-de-Calais.)*

A major portion of the North consists of the Flanders' plain which for a long time lived with the high furnaces and slag heaps of the black country cohabiting with sprawling agricultural land. Brick construction is to be seen everywhere, from the modest dwellings of workers, to public buildings, and churches, the belfries of which dot the countryside.

Lille has taken advantage of its geographical position to become one of the major European urban areas, served by ultra efficient communications i.e. the High Speed Train (TGV). However, its rich past is not forgotten, and the enhancement of its historic centre makes visible those periods when it was, in turn, Flemish, Austrian, Spanish, and finally under Louis XIV, French.

To the east at Hainaut and Cambrésis wheat and beetroot are cultivated on plains of chalk broken up by hedged valleys.

*Being 38 kilometres from the coast of England, **Calais** channels the major portion of traffic to the British Isles which use the tunnel under the Channel, or the numerous ferries. Its belfry rises to 75 metres. (Pas-de-Calais.)*

Lower Normandy

Part of Lower Normandy is the plain of Caen which is given over to wide scale cultivation and bordered to the north by a straight coast line, and the Cotentin peninsular, the northern part of the Armoricain Massif, consisting of rolling pasture land squared in by hedgerows. The west coast is of varied appearance: cliffs of granite, dunes, and beaches of sand, and the bay of the Mont-Saint-Michel. Further to the south the parkland of Normandie-Maine and the Perche are charming with their wooded hills, and small valleys.

Caen is both an industrial centre and a port which is linked to the sea by the Orne minor canal. The Abbaye aux Hommes founded by William the Conqueror in 1066, and the Abbaye aux Dames founded by his wife Mathilde, are the city's architectural jewels. At Bayeux, it is essential to see the 50 meter long tapestry created in the 11th century and which depicts the dispute of William and Harold for the crown of England.

The charming little 16th century château of **Saint-Germain-de-Livet**, *nestling amongst the thickets of Normandy is like a checkerboard of coloured stone and brick. (Calvados.)*

Honfleur, *with its old dock lined with straight and high slate dressed houses has inspired numerous painters and poets: Boudin, Corot, Baudelaire...(Calvados.)*

From **Honfleur**, with its harbour surrounded by high straight tile covered houses, to Barfleur, a charming fishing port at the very end of the Cotentin peninsular, are scattered resorts, and the long beaches selected for the landing on June 6, 1944 by the allied armies. The Pays d'Auge, a region of valleys and hedges is famous for its cheeses (Camembert, Livarot, Pont-l'évêque) and its cider.

An original site, a thousand year old history, and an architecture as beautiful as it is audacious has resulted in the **Mont-Saint-Michel** *being named a "Wonder of the West".* *(Manche.)*

To the north west of the Contentin peninsula, the **Nez de Jobourg** *is a steep headland surrounded by reefs. (Manche.)*

Upper Normandy

Upper Normandy is shared by the Seine Valley: to the north of the river lies the Pays de Caux, a chalk plateau surrounded by high cliffs, whilst the Pays de Bray is a nest of verdant pasture specialised in dairy production.

To the south the Pays d'Ouche, with its forests and pasture land, opens out onto the huge treeless plains of Neubourg and **Evreux** which are entirely given over to the growing of cereals.

*The central square at **Ferrière-sur-Risle** has picturesque old timber frame houses. (Eure.)*

Rouen, an important maritime and river port, retains from its past numerous monuments of considerable interest (the cathedral, the law courts). The "Golden Age" of the Norman Capital (middle of the 14th century – beginning of the 16th century) was a prosperous period of, in the main, merchants dealing with ship owners for trade on the new maritime routes. The port of Le Havre is a major place of trade, at the mouth of the valley of the River Seine where numerous industries are located.

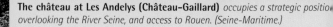

The château at Les Andelys (Château-Gaillard) *occupies a strategic position overlooking the River Seine, and access to Rouen. (Seine-Maritime.)*

Etretat, an elegant seaside resort, is surrounded by spectacular chalk cliffs. **Fécamp** is devoted to fishing and trade, whilst **Dieppe** is both the oldest of sea-side resorts in France, and has the closest beach to Paris.

The cliffs at Côte d'Albâtre and Le Tréport, *on the River Bresle estuary which marks the northern limit of Normandy. (Seine-Maritime.)*

The law courts at Rouen *were built during the "Golden Century" of the capital of Normandy (second half of the 15th century), in the Renaissance period style. (Seine-Maritime.)*

The arch known as the "Porte d'Aval et l'Aiguille" *made famous by Arsène Lupin, hero of the novel by Maurice Leblanc,* **L'Aiguille Creuse,** *are an integral part of the spectacular Cliffs at Etretat. (Seine Maritime.)*

The Loire Valley

In the north of the area the Lower Maine has a marked aspect of hedged pasture land. It could be called the Black Maine because of its houses constructed out of granite and shale, whilst the White Maine derives from the limestone soil basin of the River Huisne and River Sarthe. The old quarter of **Laval** is located on a hillside overlooking the Mayenne. **Le Mans** is a busy city (manufacturing and insurance), known world wide for its annual automobile race (the 24 Hour Race at Le Mans).

The Anjou area, which extends from both side of the Loire, between **Saumur** and Saint-Florent, is known for the mildness of its climate and the harmony of its landscape which shelters many châteaux and abbeys (Montgeoffroy, Fontevraud, Serrant, Brissac...) Washed by the waters of the River Maine, **Angers** is known for its architecture which ranges from white tufa to slate. The city deals in the famous Anjou wines, and has developed a considerable high technology industry.

The historic centre of Le Mans
has been completely restored. The "Deux-Amis" house is a typical example of Middle Age architecture. (Sarthe.)

The Brière Regional National Park, *to the north of the River Loire estuary, protects a vast marsh drained and dried by the persistent work of man. The marsh is totally accessible as a result of a network of canals. (Loire-Atlantique.)*

Epau Abbey, *close to Le Mans, was founded in 1229 by Queen Bérangère, widow of Richard the Lion Heart. The chapter room has elegant diagonal rib arches. (Sarthe.)*

Nantes, the ancient city of the Dukes of Brittany, is today the region's capital. Located at the spot where the River Loire enters the sea it had been able to trade with both Lower Brittany, the Poitou area, and more distant places. Its château, protected externally by strong towers surrounded by moats, has on the side facing the court yard an elegant Renaissance facade.

To the north of the estuary, the Grande Brière area is a vast marsh drained and dried by the persistent work of men. The Vendée has the twin attractions of both its immense beaches of white sand, and the charm of its inland country where hedged land predominates, and where the hills are sometimes crowned with wind mills. The Isle of **Noirmoutier** has the attraction of its beaches along with the offer of quiet woods, and salt marshes.

The château of Angers, *with the massive towers of its surrounding wall, is an interesting example of feudal architecture. It houses a wall covering depicting the Apocalypse, the oldest and largest (135 meters), which can only be admired. (Maine-et-Loire.)*

Saint-Gilles-Croix-de-Vie *is a community which is firmly oriented towards the sea, and where the activities of tourism and fishing exist together harmoniously. (Vendée.)*

The extent of the marshes, along with strong sunlight enables salt marsh workers to harvest salt from about a hundred kilometres of the **Noirmoutier marshes.** *(Vendée.)*

The large beach at **Sables-d'Olonne***, splendid coastal resort on the Vendée coast.*

Its mild climate, the pure Atlantic air, a preserved natural environment, along with numerous beaches make **Noirmoutier** *highly sought after by holiday makers. (Vendée.)*

Picardy

The immense extent of the Picardy plateau, interspersed with valleys and lakes, are covered with fields of cereals and beets. **Amiens** is renowned for its cathedral the dimensions of which are exceptional and result in it being the largest gothic edifice in France.

Between **Abbeville** and the sea, the bay of the **Somme** river at low tide reveals huge wild spaces covered with grass and sand, a favourite observation area for nature lovers.

To the east the department of Aisne contains the region of Thiérache with its interesting fortified churches, and the vast open spaces dominated by the cathedrals of **Laon** and **Soissons**.

Between **Compiègne** and **Senlis**, the Valois offers its forests as one of the lungs of the neighbouring Greater Paris Area. For those interested in examples of French history and architecture visits to **Pierrefonds, Compiègne, Chaalis, and Chantilly** are essential. **Beauvais**, the ancient Gallo-Roman capital, is dominated by the cathedral of Saint-Pierre, unfinished as a result of successive collapse. The choir, the vaults of which rise to almost 50 meters, has an incredibly daring style.

The Château at Chantilly *contains very valuable collections of paintings (Raphaël, Botticelli, Ingres ...) collected by the Duke of Aumale, fifth son of Louis-Philippe. (Oise.)*

Amiens Cathedral, the largest gothic building in France, has an astonishing labyrinth depicting meanders, and magnificent 16th century flamboyant stalls. (Somme.)

Soissons has retained two major architectural Middle Age religious monuments: the cathedral and abbey of Saint-Jean-des-Vignes, the extremely elegant flamboyant steeples of which can be seen from a distance across the agricultural plain which surrounds the city. (Aisne.)

Poitou-Charentes

The Poitou area consists of a plain which is drained by the tributaries of the River Loire. Here and there sheep grazed moors are to be seen. Elsewhere the fields and grassland give witness to a prosperous agriculture concentrated upon the raising of beef cattle (Charolais and Limousin), and quality dairy products along with arable production (cereals, and animal fodder).

Saint-Martin-de-Ré, *once the island's fortress, now a charming fishing port, which has kept its ancient alleyways.*

Poitiers, founded during the Gallo-Roman period, has several highly interesting monuments, including the churches of Saint-Hilaire-le-Grand, 1049, and Notre-Dame-la-Grande which is typical of the region's Roman style. The Futuroscope has available the most advanced technology in the field of communications.

Between **Niort** and La Rochelle, the Poitou marsh consisting of a dense network of canals has to be crossed before following the cove of the Aiguillon river which is festooned with oyster and mussel beds. **La Rochelle**, located between Nantes and Bordeaux faces the Atlantic Ocean and has traded with Canada, Louisiana, and the West Indies since the 18th century. Today, trawlers and pleasure boating, for which the port of Minimes has been fitted out, enliven the maritime scene.

*The entrance to the **port at La Rochelle**, a protestant stronghold when the wars of religion, from 1562 to 1598, tore the country apart is defended by the Chain and Saint Nicolas towers. Entrance to the city is via the Clock Tower Gate. (Charente-Maritime.)*

Sainte-Radegonde church at Talmont-sur-Gironde, *at the end of the fortified headland is representative of the Roman saintongeais style with its elegant chevet complimented by buttress columns. (Charente-Maritime.)*

The region of Charentes includes the old provinces of Saintonge (around **Saintes**), Angoumois (around Angoulème), and Aunis (around La Rochelle). The thirty kilometre long **island of Ré** is connected to the mainland by a huge bridge. The inhabitants of the island take full advantage of an exceptionally mild climate, producing excellent early fruit and vegetables, and long beaches bordered with pine trees attract visitors. More to the south, the island of **Oléron** charms with its wooded dunes, its beaches, and white houses.

Saintes (Roman arenas, the Abbey aux Dames), **Cognac** (the vineyards and wine storage) and **Angoulème** (the Roman cathedral), deserve visiting in depth.

*Off the coast of Oléron island is **Fort Boyard** which was constructed for surveillance of the mouth of the River Charente. It is now used as a location for filming a very popular T.V. game. (Charente-Maritime.)*

Green Venice, to the west of the Poitou marshes, is criss-crossed by a network of canals which encircle cultivated plots. Numerous villages and hamlets have a landing stage, the point of departure for a visit to the marsh. (Deux-Sèvres.)

Cognac is a universally well known liqueur, distilled from light, flavoured wines. At Cognac one can visit large storehouses where the subtle alchemy of the alcohol and the oak of the casks results in the ageing of and assemblage of this precious liquid. (Charente.)

The vaults of the ancient abbey church of Saint Savin are decorated with a remarkable collection of paintings done around 1100, the largest in France. (Vienne.)

The facade of the church of Notre Dame la Grande at Poitiers *has admirable sculpted decoration, intense life animation and depiction of the Incarnation. The church, by its proportions, is representative of Poitiers' school of Roman art. (Vienne.)*

The Cathedral of Saint Pierre at Angoulême *has a highly decorated sculpted facade which is characterised by the superimposition of arches. The whole decorated by friezes of leaves, medallions, and all varieties of animals, is full of the effect of movement. (Charente.)*

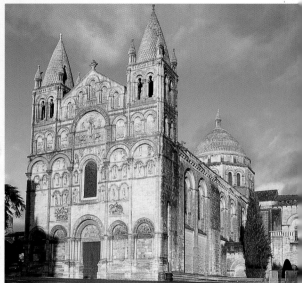

Provence
Alpes
Côte-d'Azur

Provence, crossed by the lower waters of the River Rhône, is punctuated by the outlines of the Baronnies, Ventoux, Luberon, Alpilles, Sainte-Victoire, and Sainte-Baume heights. The plains are fully cultivated: fruit, and vegetables in the Comtat Venaissin and Petite Crau areas, vines and olive trees at the foot of the Luberon and the Alpilles, with rice in the Camargue region. **Orange** (the Roman theatre), **Avignon** (the Papal Palace), **Arles** (arenas, the cloister of Saint-Trophime) and **Aix-en-Provence** (the Mirabeau square, the Place d'Albertas) are first ranking cities of art. The **Camargue,** at the heart of the Rhône delta, consists of lakes where pink flamingos stroll, and of sandy marshes roamed by herds of horses and wild cattle.

The Cistercian abbeys of Sénanque, Silvacane, and Thoronet, are interesting examples of restrained line Romanesque art.

Founded in the year 600 B.C. by the Phocaeans, **Marseilles**, throughout the centuries, has become one of the most important ports in the Mediterranean. The picturesque Vieux Port is overlooked by the Basilica of Notre-Dame-de-la-Garde.

The Abbey at Sénanque, *founded in 1148, nestles in the hollow of a lavender carpeted valley. It belongs to the considerable Cistercian order, in the same capacity as Silvacane and Le Thoronet (p. 82), its "sisters in the south of France". (Vaucluse.)*

The French Riviera (Côte d'Azur), is a point where the sea, mountains, and the sun meet marking out from **Toulon** to **Menton** a succession of dazzling beaches: with creeks, the Maures and Esterel Massifs, the gulf of Saint-Tropez, the Baie des Anges, the Riviera corniche. **Toulon**, protected by its harbour, is a major naval installation. Since the 1950s **Saint-Tropez** has been a resort of international fame, whilst **Nice**, "pearl" of the French Riviera, has a pebble beach bordered by the Promenade des Anglais along which are established the most luxurious of hotels.

Towards the north, the Alpes-de-Haute-Provence remain southern in character, whilst the massifs of the Mercantour, Queyras and Ecrins have numerous possibilities for ramblers and skiers. The highest city in Europe, **Briançon**, and gateway to the winter sports resort of Serre-Chevalier, has retained its network of fortifications. **Gap**, at the centre of a vast basin, has grown up at the junction of major communications.

The Island of Port Cros, *a classified national park, is without fear of contradiction literally one of Europe's points of paradise.*
It has an exceptional wealth of Mediterranean fauna and flora. Vehicles are forbidden, and visiting by foot is made easy by numerous indicated paths. A few discrete bays are suitable for bathing. (Var.)

The Dentelles de Montmirail, *at the foot of Mount Ventoux, are formed by curious crests of limestone standing erect in the middle of vineyards. They inspire painters, and attract numerous strollers. (Vaucluse.)*

Thoronet Abbey *is not far from the Argens valley, in the middle of wooded hills. Built during the second half of the 12th century its buildings are an example of Cistercian architectural sobriety.*
(Var.)

The Colorado de Rustrel, *not far from Apt, is formed from ancient ochre quarries , a mixture of sandy clay and iron oxide. The Vaucluse produces 3,000 tons of ochre annually. this is used in the preparation of paint, and distemper. (Vaucluse.)*

Albertas Square
*(17th and 18th centuries),
historic centre
of Aix-en-Provence.
(Bouches-du-Rhône.)*

The Roman Theatre at Vaison-la-Romaine,
which can accommodate 6,000 spectators. (Vaucluse.)

*80,000 spectators came to view the gladiators fight
in the* **Arles Arenas** *built during the reign of Augustus.
(Bouches-du-Rhône.)*

The old village of **Baux de Provence** *Citadel in
the Alpilles. (Bouches-du-Rhône.)*

Provence-Alpes-Côte-d'Azur

Seasonal migration in the Clarée Valley, *near Briançon, which has without doubt the most balanced and hospitable of landscapes in the Dauphinoise mountain area. (Hautes-Alpes.)*

The Esterel Massif seen from Cabris, *near Grasse. Like the Maures Massif, more to the east, for the most part it is covered with fire threatened forests (pine, oak). (Alpes-Maritimes, Var.)*

Saint-Véran, *in the Queyras area, is the highest village in Europe. At more than 2,000 metres, its chalets are grouped together on a well exposed south facing terrace. (Hautes-Alpes.)*

Villefranche-sur-Mer, *both a fishing port and seaside resort, it is located in the hollow of a magnificent harbour overlooked by wooded hills. It has kept its citadel, built at the end of the 16th century by the Duke of Savoy, and the old streets around the marina. (Alpes-Maritimes.)*

During the International Film Festival, in May, cinema lovers and photographers wait in front of **Cannes' palace** *like hotels for the appearance of big screen stars. (Alpes-Maritimes.)*

Provence-Alpes-Côte-d'Azur

Rhône-Alpes

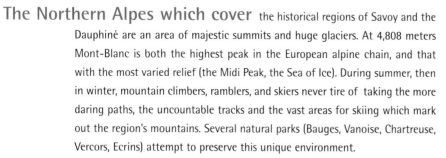

The Northern Alpes which cover the historical regions of Savoy and the Dauphiné are an area of majestic summits and huge glaciers. At 4,808 meters Mont-Blanc is both the highest peak in the European alpine chain, and that with the most varied relief (the Midi Peak, the Sea of Ice). During summer, then in winter, mountain climbers, ramblers, and skiers never tire of taking the more daring paths, the uncountable tracks and the vast areas for skiing which mark out the region's mountains. Several natural parks (Bauges, Vanoise, Chartreuse, Vercors, Ecrins) attempt to preserve this unique environment.

Located at the confluence of the Isére and the Drac, **Grenoble** has become the financial and intellectual capital of the Alpes. **Chambéry, Aix-les-Bains**, and **Annecy**, close to the Bourget and Annecy lakes ensure their inhabitants an enviable lifestyle.

At the foot of the Alpes lies Dombes a clay plateau scattered with hundreds of lakes.

Beyond the Saône river the heights of Beaujolais are covered with vines which produce a fresh fruity red wine. Further to the west, at Forez, verdant fields and grass lands are to be found up to a height of 1,000 meters, above are forests of pine and beech, and high stripped stubble. **Saint-Etienne** is to be found at the start of the Forez plain, it has ceased mining for coal, and diversified its activities.

Lyon, superbly located where the River Rhône and Saône meet has taken advantage of its geographical position to become a prosperous regional metropolis, and first ranking university and medical research establishment.

From Valentinois to the Montélimar basin, the Rhône Valley alternates, between orchards and vineyards, in a huge cultivated patchwork.

To the south of Valence, the Rhône runs between the Vivarais, at the edge of the Massif Central shaped by erosion (numerous natural curiosities) and the Vercors, a high limestone plateau hollowed out by water.

The Vercors, *a high limestone plateau, was gouged by rivers. Roads are sometimes dug even into the sides, and numerous paths for strolling criss-cross the mountain. (Isère, Drôme.)*

At the foot of Mount Granier, *on the eastern exposed slopes which overlook the River Isère, thrives a vast vineyard which takes advantage of the first rays of the sun. (Isère, Savoie.)*

The Midi Peak *(3,842 metres) launche its formidable wall of rock above the Chamonix valley.(Haute-Savoie.)*

Between Vercors and Provence, the Diois massif consists of a succession of crests and hollows. (Drôme.)

*Between the valleys of Romanche and Vénéon, the **Deux-Alpes** have a huge area for skiing, and lots of sunshine for skiers. (Isère.)*

The Gorges de l'Ardèche *which can be visited by canoe, or kayak, have profoundly eaten into the plateau of the lower Vivarais. (Ardèche.)*

Between the rivers Saône and Loire, **Charlieu** has for a long time played an important commercial role. Today the city is specialised in the weavimg of silk, and the hosiery trade. Its Benedictine abbey, founded in 870, then incorporated into Cluny, had its Roman cloister rebuilt during the 15th century.

On the hillsides which overlook the River Saône, to the north of Lyon, the grape has been cultivated since Roman times. They produce fruity, red, wines which are best drank when young. The Beaujolais Villages exists as follows: Morgon, Chiroubles, Juliénas, Moulin-à-vent, Fleurie, Chénas, Côte-de-Brouilly, Brouilly, Régnié, and Saint-Amour. Before the development of improved means of transport, Lyon, was the main outlet for this wine, to the point that the city was, as the joke goes is, "watered by three rivers: the Rhône, the Saône, and the Beaujolais". (Saône-et-Loire.)

The cathedral of Saint Jean at Lyon, *se commenced during the 12th century, has a gothic facade the portals of which have retained a very ornate early 14th century decor. (Rhône.)*

The choir of Brou Church *(suburbs of Bourg-en-Bresse), built by Margaret of Austria from 1506, houses numerous tombs which mark the high point of Flemish sculpture in Burgundy. Tomb of Margaret of Austria. (Ain.)*

Overseas France

Guadeloupe and Martinique, each of which being separate regions, are volcanic islands located between the Atlantic ocean and the Caribbean. Apart from the exotic clichés about the beaches, coconut trees, and West Indian music, they are endeavouring to add to the resources of tourism by economic diversification to compensate for the slow decline in sugar cane.

To the north of Brazil, beside the Atlantic, **Guyana** is, for the most part, covered with tropical forest. Its subsoil is rich (bauxite, gold) and tourism is in the process of being developed. The Aerospace Centre at Kourou is responsible for launching the Ariane European Rocket.

The island of **Réunion** is located in the Indian Ocean, off shore from Madagascar. It is characterised by its volcanic outline (Piton de la Fournaise, 2,631 meters), and a temperate tropical climate suitable for the cultivation of sugar cane, vanilla, and plants for the manufacture of perfume. Magnificent scenery, and the attraction of the sea make it a favourite destination for tourists throughout the entire year.

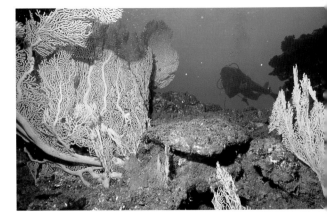

Off the coast of Réunion, *a dive under a sea of incredible wealth. (La Réunion.)*
Ph. E. Dutrieux.

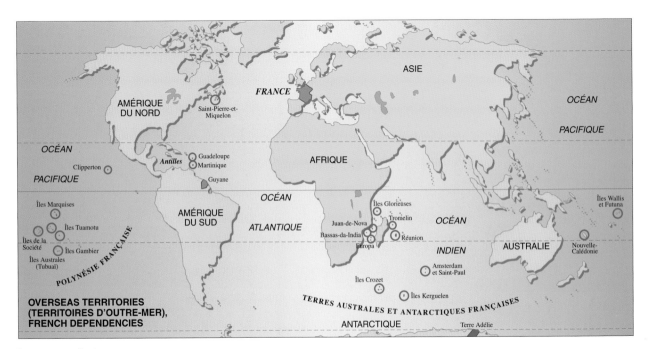

OVERSEAS TERRITORIES
(TERRITOIRES D'OUTRE-MER),
FRENCH DEPENDENCIES

Off the coast of Guadeloupe, **the Saintes' archipelago** *has kept intact the ma or part of its idyllic landscape.* *(Guadeloupe.)*

Overseas Territories include **New Caledonia**, Melanesian islands whose main resources, other than tourism, are nickel and forestry, **Polynesia** with Tahiti and the Marchesas with idyllic landscapes, and **Mayotte**, small island in the Comoros in the Indian Ocean.

Anses–d'Arlets, *facing the Caribbean, is a charming fishing village which has retained its traditional huts. (Martinique.)*

Index

First cover page: *Etretat Cliffs (Seine-Maritime) ; Château de Chambord (Loir-et-Cher) ; Pays de Cize in the Basque country (Pyrénées-Atlantiques)
Pont du Gard (Gard) ; The Pyrenees Mountain Chain (Hautes-Pyrénées) ; Sénanque Abbey (Vaucluse)*

Fourth cover page: *The Cathedral of Notre-Dame (Paris).*

Cartography: Patrick Mérienne - Photoengraving: Nord Compo, Villeneuve d'Ascq

© 2001, 2008 Éditions Ouest-France, Edilarge S.A., Rennes
Cet ouvrage a été achevé d'imprimer par l'imprimerie Pollina, Luçon (85) - L45026
I.S.B.N. 978-2-7373-4361-2 - N° d'éditeur : 5544-01-03-01-08
Dépôt légal : janvier 2008
www.editionsouestfrance.fr